CO-ATV-779

Jim Aylward's

Things No One Ever Tells You

97,27,55, 89 *handwritten notes*

WARNER BOOKS

A Warner Communications Company

IT'S THE TRUTH,
THE WHOLE TRUTH AND NOTHING
BUT THE TRUTH
but it took Jim Aylward
to tell you such famous facts as . . .
GRINGLISH IS NOW "SPOKE" IN MANY
PLACES AROUND THE WORLD. Travelers find
signs now in East Berlin hotel cloakrooms reading
"Please hang yourself here!" A Dutch bulb
catalogue offers mail order buyers "a speedy execution." A bread bakery in Bombay says "We are
number one loafers . . . best in whole town."
An Istanbul hotel room sign reads "To call room
service, please to open door and call room service."
And a Mexican hotel requests "Please hang your
order before retiring on your doorknob."

IT'S ONE OF THE THINGS YOU NEVER
THOUGHT YOU'D KNOW, FROM JIM
AYLWARD, whose humor is well-known from his
syndicated newspaper column "Jim Aylward's
Journal" and his top-rated New York radio
programs on WRFM. He is also the author of
You're Dumber In The Summer, a book
of fun facts for young readers.

Dedication

To any listener or reader
who has never written me a letter
of complaint.

Acknowledgments

In putting together a compilation of facts such as this, many people and organizations play a part. While most of this material is based on actual news stories and data as reported in the public press, I would like to acknowledge the help of the National Geographic Society, United Press International and Associated Press.

In addition may I thank writer-researcher David Godwin for his valuable contributions, my beautiful secretary Jean Cuccinello and my encouraging and enthusiastic friends, John C. Moler and Norma Sams.

Some of these "things" appeared in a slightly different form in *Leaders* magazine and are used here with the kind permission of its President and Editor-in-Chief Henry O. Dormann.

—Jim Aylward, New York, 1981

Jim Aylward's

Things No One Ever Tells You

Prologue

I have always hated books with prologues and I often wondered why they were there. Is the author paid by the word and the more words in the book the more money in the pocket? Or is it that so many famous writers have written prologues over the years that publishers think every great tome should have one? Well, whatever the reason, I will not break tradition. This book has a prologue too. Huh? Only novels or plays can have prologues? Really? Then this will be the first non-fiction work with a prologue! It gives me one more page and under the terms of my contract I get hospitalization benefits if I turn in enough lines. And they're neatly typed.

Chapter One

The chapter that answers the question "How did a tall, good-looking young son of a gun of a guy from Stoneham, Massachusetts get involved in the tawdry, sometimes evil, always questionable world of trivia?" The answer is, it all started at the age of eleven when he wrote a book in longhand called *How Silly Can You Get?* That book was never published. Today, in sleazy, dimly-lit rooms in God forsaken parts of the world, international collectors of weird writing read that manuscript in faded photo copies, trying to understand the hidden aspects of those child-like phrases that over the years have become ripe and meaningless. And now, fully grown and strikingly unmanageable, he emerges as America's foremost authority on

11

minutiae. (*Actually, it's the same kind of stuff I wrote when I was a kid, but now Warners has agreed to publish it! Where did they go wrong?*)

IN ANCIENT ARABIA people who bathed regularly were tax exempt. The plan was designed to get more Arabians into hot water.

AT THE AGE OF FORTY-TWO, PRINTER BENJAMIN FRANKLIN had an income of $100,000. Poor Richard wasn't.

IRAN HAS SET UP SOMETHING CALLED THE BUREAU TO STOP BAD ACTS. That's not, by the way, in direct response to Chuck Barris, but to show they mean business, they're closing down the world's oldest business. Tehran's red-light district, considered to be the biggest in the Middle East before the revolution, is to be demolished. In its place? An Islamic bazaar with a mosque. The women there, says the government, will be taught *handicrafts*.

GEORGE WASHINGTON predicted each year that he wouldn't live until his next birthday. He died while taking his own pulse.

NEARLY HALF THE MEN WHO GO TO SINGLES BARS aren't.

THE EFFECT OF CAFFEINE on your central nervous system is strongest during the first hour after your morning coffee or tea, but the effect persists two to three hours later.

EATING MARGARINE INSTEAD OF BUTTER can add two and a half years to your life. Doctors at the University of Leuven in Belgium say the margarine's chief advantage is that it cuts down on heart disease.

THE JAW MUSCLE is the one that can work longest without getting tired. Your Avon lady is living proof of that.

QUEEN ISABELLA of Spain lived from 1451 to 1504 and is said to have had only two baths during that time. She used an awful lot of powder.

THE UNITED STATES GOVERNMENT employs three times as many civilians as AT&T.

THE GOSSARD COMPANY OF NEW YORK is out with a new item designed for the female executive. Called "Going Places," it's a portable, packageable nightgown that can be carried in a purse. The company says it's ideal for business women or any woman who needs a quick change. *Sure.*

NEXT TIME YOU'RE IN TUCSON, ARIZONA notice there are no potholes. You may find holes in the streets, but in Tucson they're called *pavement deficiencies*.

IN CASE YOU'RE MAKING ANY PLANS, scientists at the University of California say a major breakthrough in quasar research has convinced them the universe will collapse in about seventy billion years.

IN 1776 a person could expect to live to be thirty-five.

A NUDE BEACH IS NOT AN EASY PLACE TO PICK UP A DATE. It's actually harder to meet members of the opposite sex in the nude than when you're wearing your bathing suit. And holding in your stomach muscles until you turn blue.

IN JOHANNESBURG, CITY BUS DRIVERS are given a bonus each month if they manage to refrain from attacking the passengers.

IN BAR HARBOR, MAINE at the Jackson Laboratory there are three mice that look like mice and act like mice but are more than mice. They're a mixture of mice and men. They look like animals but they're a little human. They're partly derived from cells containing a human chromosome. John Steinbeck becomes reality.

BARBARA FORD, author of the book *Future Food,* predicts we'll all be eating insects by the year 2000 and loving it. Miss Ford says if you have a craving for peanut butter, a spider sandwich gives the same taste without the stickiness. Until 2000 skip the spider and stick to Skippy.

WHEN YOU SHOP FOR FRUIT NEVER PINCH A PEAR. Pear pinching causes brown spots. Even Esoterica won't get them out.

YOUR FACE LIFT is supposed to last five to ten years. After that doctors say you may need a mini lift. Or a maxi mask.

RYE BREAD IS MOST POPULAR WITH-OUT SEEDS. Levy's famous New York bakery makes sixty-five percent unseeded rye. The rest is seeded. See?

CINNAMON IS POISON if ingested in large amounts. That's why it's so hard to get a cinnamon bagel.

THE CHEETAH IS THE FASTEST RUN-NER in the animal kingdom. A cheetah can go sixty miles an hour. My '67 Cougar won't even do that!

THE MOST EXPENSIVE WRITING PA-PER in the world is $8,000 for 100 sheets. Cart it away from Cartier.

A SYMPOSIUM today is an instructive and serious affair. Originally, however, the word meant "drinking together." In Ancient Greece it was a catered party at which from three to nine guests would eat, drink, and be entertained by musicians, jugglers, and courtesans. That brawl you attended last night was a symposium.

Chapter Two

In this chapter the devastating truth about the author's life is finally revealed. For years it was talked about in smoky, foul-aired parlors of the night. It was whispered. It was muttered. It was hidden. Secret. Mysterious. And then, not being able to face the light of day, not having an honest answer for the questioning faces of his time, this slit-eyed, tanned, taut muscled young whip from the east, opened the door and allowed the wondering world to witness at last the past he had tried so valiantly to disguise. "Hell," he said, "I'll even tell Merv Griffin! I don't care anymore!" Summoning up all the courage in his aching loins, taking a last deep breath of smoky, polluted air, he said, "I've tried to hide it, but I can't any longer. The truth is . . .

I'm an ... *infotainer!*" (*I've been an infotainer all my life, really. Information and entertainment! I could never keep my hands off them! And today, since nobody cares anymore, I'm writing this book and I'll be rich and famous! Maybe with the royalties I can get some therapy.*)

QUEEN VICTORIA'S CHEF was very careful about how much garlic he put in her salad. He would chew a raw clove of the stuff and then breathe on her royal vegetables. He served it, of course, with his famous Halitosis Dressing.

TWENTY YEARS AGO the Hollywood Women's Press Club presented Ronald Reagan with the title of "World's Most Sincere Actor."

ONLY IN ALGERIA can you pay your court fine in beer. That'll be two six-packs and a quart.

THE FAMOUS STRESS AUTHORITY, DR. HANS SELYE, says, "Stress never depends on what happens to you, but on how you take it." Working hard at a job you like probably will not produce harmful stress. An easier assignment you really hate could do you in.

A FACTORY IN CZECHOSLOVAKIA has come up with a new way to cut the time lost to coffee breaks. They're selling employees half-size cigarettes.

THE DAY IS ON THE WAY WHEN PILOTS will be in direct communication with computers on the ground via electrodes attached to their heads. Dr. Carl Sem-Jacobsen, a Norwegian Brain Institute researcher, believes direct communication between the pilot's brain and the computer would improve greatly the reliability of data transferred between the two. That would really be an automatic pilot.

WHEN YOU MEET SOMEONE YOU LIKE your eyebrows fly up.

NON-SMOKERS ingest from food, water, and air a baseline level of cancer-causing agents equivalent to smoking two cigarettes a day.

THERE ARE EXACTLY 332 DIMPLES on your golf ball. Count them.

DWIGHT DAVID EISENHOWER wasn't that president's real name. He was born David Dwight Eisenhower.

A MOTEL CHAIN IN QUEENSLAND, AUSTRALIA offers a special honeymooner's package. Children can stay at the place at no extra charge.

THE GREEK WORD FOR HANGOVER is *crapula*. The Greek cure for that ailment used to be rubbing half a lemon under your arm.

AN EXOTIC DANCER takes exactly one hour to shake off 144 calories. I have long hours of research on that.

WHEN THE MAKERS OF A BRITISH DETERGENT called Square Deal Surf stopped advertising, reduced price, and increased weight, sales went down sharply. When they resumed advertising, reduced the amount in the box, and raised the price, sales went up.

YOUR WORKING LIFE HAS IN-CREASED BY NINE YEARS, but your life expectancy has jumped by eighteen years. That gives you an extra nine years just to fool around.

A SURVEY OF THE TYPE OF PERSON MOST LIKELY TO LIE shows politicians finish just a step ahead of children under six.

ABRAHAM LINCOLN had a rose tatoo.

THE PERSON WHO WHISTLES AND SINGS while he works doesn't get as much done as the one who's constantly griping. The person who's always moaning about the job, the company, and the management is the one who puts out the most work.

RUSSIAN DOCTORS say adding lecithin to a diet can help dissolve gallstones. Of the patients treated with lecithin most had reductions in pain. One or two tablespoons a day of either granular or liquid lecithin does it.

IN RIO de JANIERO it's against the law to dance the samba in a tunnel.

JACK THE RIPPER was left handed.

ARABS stroke their beards when they see a pretty girl. Italians pull an earlobe. The English shyly look away.

QUEEN ELIZABETH burns all her old clothes in the royal furnace. Did you expect a yard sale?

IN A TEST at the Louisiana State University School of Dentistry it was found that orange juice was far more effective at eating away tooth enamel than diet or regular soft drinks. Do you suppose Anita Bryant has caps?

THE AVERAGE OFFICE WORKER spends two full weeks a year on coffee breaks. The rest of the time, of course, is spent making personal phone calls, having a smoke, and taking home paper clips, ribbons, pens, and file folders.

THEY HAVE A SIMPLE SOLUTION IN ITALY for what to do with buildings constructed without proper permits. They blow them up.

THERE'S A 103-YEAR-OLD BAKER IN YUGOSLAVIA who says he has made love to exactly 4,320 women in his lifetime. He knows that because he kept a perfect written record. Just imagine what he could have accomplished if he'd had a calculator.

IF YOU WANT TO AVOID HIGH BLOOD PRESSURE take off your clothes. The American Heart Association tested residents of a nudist camp for two years and found fewer persons with high blood pressure than the average. Only seven percent had high blood pressure compared with a national average of seventeen percent. One woman at the camp says, "When people come in here, they forget their troubles." As long as they remember where they put their hats.

THE AVERAGE WOMAN TODAY kisses seventy-nine men before she gets married. Number eighty has to watch it!

IN SWITZERLAND you can be fined for tax evasion but they won't ever send you to jail for it.

THE MOST POPULAR DRINK IN THE WORLD today besides water is tea.

EVERYTIME YOU LAUGH you burn up three and a half calories.

TWO HUNDRED YEARS AGO women put their wedding rings on their thumbs. It looked nice when they were hitch-hiking West.

THE NUMBER ONE CAUSE OF HEART ATTACKS IN MEN OVER SIXTY is women under thirty.

Chapter Three

The part of the book that covers those impossible-to-forget years in which the author, grimy, dirt covered, bearded, and bleary eyed, struggled through the mud-soaked valleys of Korea, in the bowels of the Bowling Alley, the peaks of Pork Chop, wearily telling his buddies, his superiors, even his enemies, of which there were legion, that he was, after all, a star. "Dammit," he said. "I had my own radio show in Lynn, Massachusetts! And look at me now—eating Thanksgiving dinner in the wrong half of a mess kit with ice cream on my stuffing and one soup spoon!" While he insisted he was a star, he was really the star who carried the BAR, the Browning Automatic Rifle. "I carried that sucker for a full year!" he complains gruffly.

"Once I got the barrel of it in the mud and I tried to dislodge the mud with my finger and lodged my finger. There I was in the middle of the war with my finger up my rifle." (*Actually, I said to myself at that grimy, dirt covered low point in my life, "Jim, someday you'll put this in a paperback for Warners and you son-of-a-gun, you'll be fingering a typewriter instead!"*)

JULIA CHILD drives a Volkswagen.

SHELLEY WINTERS real name is Shirley Schrift. Which is easy for *her* to say.

A KISS HAS AT LEAST TWENTY-FIVE CALORIES. A molasses kiss, that is. Any calories in the torrid kind are burned up fast.

MEN SELDOM MAKE PASSES AT GIRLS WHO WEAR GLASSES, but they hire them faster when they're job hunting. Glasses give the impression that a woman is business-like and intelligent.

THE FAMOUS NAVY SALUTE over a grave was originally designed to drive away evil spirits as they escaped from the hearts of the dead. It was thought that the doors to men's hearts stood ajar at such times permitting devils to enter. The three volleys fired into the air were supposed to frighten the devils away.

JOHN DEWAR CALLED HIS WHISKEY "WHITE LABEL" because at the time he first made it he couldn't afford color print.

A REPORT FROM THE UNIVERSITY OF MICHIGAN says thirty-nine is the age at which we all start to shrink, creak or break. Jack Benny was right.

EDWIN C. BLISS, author of "Getting Things Done," says, "Of all the time-saving techniques ever developed, perhaps the most effective of all is frequent use of the word, 'No!' "

TODAY IT'S NEW YORK, but 1000 years ago Cahokia was the largest city in what is now the USA. The Indian settlement had a population of about 30,000 and was located in what is now Southern Illinois.

THOUGH COLUMBIA IS BEST KNOWN FOR COFFEE, more than 600 mines make it a leader in gold production. Colombia also mines ninety percent of the world's emeralds.

WILD TURKEYS HAVE LESS MEAT BUT MORE BRAINS. Wild brains, however.

MOTOROLA HAS DEVELOPED A TELEPHONE you lug around with you. It's small enough to fit into your briefcase or your back pocket. It's like a walkie-talkie except it's a real phone that really works. You don't need a limo. You just walk along the avenue talking into your pocket.

MORE THAN 1400 ACRES OF FARM- LAND in Fayette County, Iowa is owned by three corporations based in Liechtenstein.

CARL SANDBERG WENT TO WEST POINT. But only for a short time. He left after he flunked English.

R.J. REYNOLDS is working on cigarettes made from cereal grains. Sorghum, rice, wheat, and the like. In the future you can snap, crackle, and puff.

A DRUG TO FIGHT ANGINAL PAIN coupled with plain aspirin seems to be whipping migraine headache. A study from the University of Texas says aspirin combined with dipyrida- mole is effective and safer than most standard therapy.

THAT VERY SPECIAL HOUSE DRESS- ING you like so much at your favorite restau- rant's salad bar is mostly made by Kraft. The restaurant buys it by the can.

IF YOU WAKE UP WITH A HANGOVER and you didn't have a thing to drink, chances are you've worked too hard and stayed up too late.

IF YOU HAVE VERY DARK HAIR some experts say it means you have an intense per- sonality. If you have light hair you enjoy a good time. Blondes *do* have more fun. If you have an intense personality and you're blonde, only your hairdresser knows for sure.

IF YOU CHEW ON THE CENTERFOLD OF YOUR FAVORITE MAGAZINE you may get lead poisoning. Dr. Dan Jenkins of Sonoma State Hospital in California reports a link between magazines, lead poisoning, and mental illness. Don't nibble *Newsweek!* Don't munch *McCall's!*

SCIENTISTS SAY OLDER WOMEN tend to retain their overall intelligence longer than older men. They also tend to hide cash in their bunny slippers.

FORTY-FIVE TO SIXTY MILLION PEO-PLE believe they have sleeping problems. Ten million see a doctor for it. Half of them get sleeping pills.

THE PONY EXPRESS letter rate was five dollars per half-ounce. And you thought twenty cents was too much.

THE MOST EXPENSIVE SEASONING today is saffron. $700 a pound wholesale.

IF YOU'RE THE AVERAGE AMERICAN you drank twenty-four gallons of beer last year. That was *some* party!

THE MOST USED PUBLIC TELE-PHONE in New York City is the one at the

Penn Station Concourse between tracks twenty and twenty-one.

WHEN YOU FLY TO ARGENTINA today bring some of that stuff Mr. Whipple squeezes on TV. The airports there now charge you for it.

AT THE HEIGHT OF THE VIETNAM WAR the United States had one admiral or general for each 2600 men. Now, in this so-called *peacetime*, there is an admiral or general for every 1800 men. Waging peace is hell.

EVERYTIME YOU BUY A FROZEN DINNER you're paying eight to ten dollars a pound for the meat in those foil wrapped meals. Foiled again.

PEANUT BUTTER MUST CONTAIN NINETY PERCENT PEANUTS. Those peanut spreads give you much less peanuts and a lot more spread. Whatever that is.

SPEAKING OF SPREAD, middle-aged men are the most attractive males of any age group. I certainly hope so.

SEVENTY-ONE PERCENT OF ALL WIVES today wear sheer nightgowns to bed.

Twenty-four percent wear those cotton pyjamas. The other five percent? They wear very natural expressions.

THE WORD "BRIDE" derives from the ancient Teutonic word meaning "to cook."

THE CREEKS THAT SURROUND LITTLE SOLDIER MOUNTAIN in Idaho are called Pistol, Winchester, Colt, Lugar, Automatic, '38, '45, and Popgun.

THE SANDPIPER CAN HEAR LOW FREQUENCY SOUND traveling thousands of miles. In fact, flying high above the Mississippi River, the sandpiper can hear the surf from both the Atlantic and Pacific coasts.

THE FATTEST NEWSPAPER EVER PRINTED was the *New York Times* Sunday October 17, 1965. It had 946 pages and weighed seven and a half pounds.

THE 34,000 PEOPLE WHO LIVE IN BEVERLY HILLS hire 134,000 full-time servants and keep 600 resident doctors busy. And the fire department requests you call them at least three weeks in advance of any fire.

Chapter Four

The moment that at last brings into focus the blurred image of that hazy, still October morning in New Hampshire when the author encountered the aliens for the first time. True, he had been hitting the Perrier in Portsmouth and his sinewy frame was sinfully tired at the time, but there could be no denying their appearance. They surrounded his '67 Cougar with unrelenting, bone chilling light and demanded he follow them to their craft, a reconditioned DC-10. Once inside the author was zapped with rays of neon so strong his considerable brain felt whipped into Jell-O. And then the question came from the aliens. The same question that had been asked him countless times by numberless faces in faceless places the world over

... "Where do you get all these 'Things No One Ever Tells You'?" The tight-lipped, jut-jawed author, his Jell-O brains boiling boundlessly, said what he has said so many times to so many people: "Buzz off!"

When he came to he was alone in the Cougar and the FM radio was blasting "Close Encounters of The Third Kind" by the Living Strings. "Those ——— Living Strings!" he shouted into the cold, gray countryside. "They follow me wherever I go! Will I never be free of them?"

It was then that he realized his mind no longer felt like Jell-O. But he couldn't deny he felt like a pizza. With sausage and green peppers.

ASPIRIN WAS DISCOVERED EIGHTY-ONE YEARS AGO, never approved by the FDA and today Americans take fifty billion tablets a year.

KAY KYSER, the famous band leader, never played a musical instrument.

DINOSAURS ranged from the size of a chicken to the size of a five-story building.

CHARLES ATLAS, the world's most perfectly developed man, as he called himself, wasn't really called Charles Atlas. He was really named Angelo Siciliano.

EARLY AMERICANS SOMETIMES NAMED PLACES FOR THINGS that ailed them. There's Belly Ache, South Carolina; Appendicitis Hill, Idaho; Sore Fingers, Arizona; and Sore Thumb, Washington.

FOUR OUT OF EVERY TEN SCREWDRIVERS are bought by women. Not the orange juice kind. The other kind.

THERE ARE 600,000 DOGS IN NEW YORK CITY.

THERE ARE 1,000 DIFFERENT KINDS OF FLEAS. As Jonathan Swift said, "So naturalists observe, a flea hath smaller fleas that on him prey and these have smaller still to bite 'em ... and so proceed ad infinitum." That's what Jonathan said. It never got a big yuk but then Swift wasn't exactly boffo in 1733. He's not boffo today here either.

IN MIDDLE EUROPEAN COUNTRIES during the eighteenth century, when a woman finally managed to snare a husband she never had to bathe again. Just a little mutton juice behind each ear and she was presentable.

BABIES LIKE TO YAWN A LOT. They yawn more than mothers and fathers, except maybe at three in the morning.

THE PEOPLE WHO MAKE HAIR-PIECES for men say their biggest customers are salesmen and men in advertising. After that comes public relations men, teachers, and bankers.

ALMOST ALL ASTRONAUTS AND STRIPTEASE ARTISTS are first born children. That just proves the first born really takes off.

YOU CAN GO A LONG WAY ON THE FOOD YOU EAT. You're not just living on the food of today or even yesterday. In some cases, doctors say you live on food eaten as long as fourteen days ago. Oh, I hope not ... that was the weekend I had that chili!

IF YOU'VE BEEN TAKING A BLUE VALIUM before each conference with the boss, check out the new drug that can actually increase your intelligence. *American Druggist* magazine reports PRL-8-53 has enabled test subjects to increase their powers of recall and memory considerably. The day is coming when you'll be able to smarten up just by popping a pill.

TO PREVENT A HEART ATTACK a British scientist says don't bring home the bacon, bring home the seafood. Dr. John Vane of the Wellcome Laboratories in London says fish contain a chemical acid which helps produce another chemical in your body that helps prevent blood clots. He says Eskimos eat more fish than anyone and rarely get heart attacks. Scallops and oysters contain the biggest percentage of the anti-clotting substance.

IF THERE'S NO TV IT MUST BE THURSDAY IN ICELAND. The television free day is designed to reduce disruption of family life. Radio Iceland loves it.

EARTHWORMS WERE ONCE CONSIDERED AN ALL AROUND WONDER DRUG in Iran. They were baked and eaten with bread to reduce the size of a bladder stone.

SMITH IS NOT THE MOST COMMON FAMILY NAME in the world today. Johnson and Jones aren't topping the list, either. Seventy-five million people call themselves Chang.

IF YOU TAKE A BATH EACH DAY Dr. Berd Rudiger Balda says you may be too clean to be good. The University of Munich professor says we all wash too much today, bathing away good bacteria and allowing bad bugs to rash us. He insists Queen Elizabeth I had the right idea when she said she took a bath once a month whether she needed it or not.

A HUNGARIAN MAGAZINE polled 800 people between the ages of fourteen and thirty and only ten percent knew who Nikita Khrushchev was. Over a third thought he was the first man in space. He wasn't.

SCIENTISTS AT SWEDEN'S Institute of Molecular Crytogenetics have crossed a human with a carrot, fusing human cell cultures with cells from carrots. The researchers say the differences between humans and carrots aren't all that great. One day soon your favorite rock star may be a vegetable.

SOUTH AFRICAN RADIO reports rats are now being bred for food in Ghana, Nigeria, and the Ivory Coast. They call it "alternative meat sources." I call it *rat-atouille*.

RESEARCHERS AT SAN DIEGO STATE UNIVERSITY say if you exercise regularly and vigorously you can help stall mental deterioration. That can start, they say, when you're an old fool of twenty-five.

Chapter Five

Within this chapter the author tells of his long, tawdry, sleazy, and, of course, utterly successful career in radio; full-bosomed women on the telephone wanting his voice, days and nights behind the mike mesmerizing millions with his monotone, ad-libbing traffic reports when there was no helicopter and often no traffic, playing "It's Impossible" and calling it "The Way Of Love" (he always secretly believed they were the same song!) and titillating town after town with his tirade of talk. Starting out as a young, cool, casual, carefree, incredibly-even featured fellow with a sense of the ridiculous, he travels the tedious trail of trivia to its ultimate end, New York City, with its limos and limelight, it's takers and fakers, its high times and low life.

(One night in the heavy heat of August, I was at a penthouse party overlooking the water towers and fire escapes of this magnificent city I love. I raised my glass high in a salute to her twinkling lights and I said, "New York, you'll get me yet!" The tiny full-bosomed nymph next to me laughed a twinkling, tinkling New York laugh, put her nymphlike hand in mine and said, "Henry Morgan said that on a penthouse terrace in '75.")

PEOPLE AGED FORTY TO SIXTY ARE THE MOST IRRITABLE. That's what kids on the corner say, anyhow.

PAGE AMERICA AND UNITED AIRLINES are working on an in-flight telephone system. Soon you can make a phone call from high in the sky. If the connection is a little ethereal that will just enhance your image. After all, you told them you walk on water. The least you can do is call them from heaven.

JAPANESE TOURISTS LOVE TO VISIT THE USA, but they have one little complaint.

When they get their souvenirs home they find them all carefully stamped "MADE IN JAPAN."

THE SOVIET UNION increased the sale of camel meat to help consumers get over the hump during the United States grain boycott. "I'll have a humpburger please, and a vodka tonic."

ONLY ONE OF EVERY SIX MILLION ADULTS has achieved the sort of fame that get them mentioned in the history books.

BRITISH WOMEN ARE GETTING BUSTIER and doctors are blaming it on the birth control pill. Physicians at London University say the pill enlarges breasts by two inches. Berlei Limited, the undergarment company, agrees, saying sales of super C and D cups are up. Double D cups have doubled.

WITH LUCK THE RAVEN CAN LIVE TO BE FORTY years old. That's an old bird. But after forty, nevermore, nevermore.

WHAT DO AMERICAN MEN AND WOMEN DO MOST FREQUENTLY with their leisure time? Uh uh. *That's* number two. Number one is ... they eat. Other high ranking activities include watching TV, listening to radio and to records at home.

IN POLAND THEY NEVER TELL POLISH JOKES. They like Russian jokes better. A current favorite at smart lunches is the question "What is the definition of a chamber quartet?" The answer is "The Moscow Philharmonic after a tour of the USA."

THERE IS NO SUCH THING as a genuine earthquake prediction. However, the United States now has the National Earthquake Prediction Evaluation Council. When somebody figures out how to predict an earthquake this council, already in operation, will evaluate them. In the meantime, they are evaluating the fact there is no prediction to evaluate.

IF YOU HAVE MORE THAN ONE CHERUB, the angelic creatures are not cherubs. They are cherubim.

HARRY HOUDINI, the giant of magicians, was actually five feet, one-half inches tall. The Alan Ladd of escape artists.

WOMEN HAVE THINNER EAR DRUMS THAN MEN DO. They're able to hear higher notes. Anything you can hear she can hear higher.

ESKIMOS DO BUY REFRIGERATORS. They use them to keep foods from freezing.

IF YOU'RE THE KIND OF LOVER who likes the touchy-feely closeness that often is missing in a telephone call, then your bed table needs Feel-a-Phone. International Resource Development Inc. has invented a telephone complete with a handy dandy hand. The hand isn't real, but then what do you want for $5,000? Your mechanical hand will transmit gestures to another Feel-a-Phone hand at the end of the line. Break off a relationship from New York and they can wave goodbye from Seattle. If a wave isn't sufficient, there are fifty-nine other gestures to use. Four fingers, one thumb.

BEFORE YOU DECIDE TO PUNCH YOUR PARTNER IN THE MOUTH, better check the British medical journal *Lancet*. They're reporting that since many people carry bacteria on their teeth (partners are notorious for it!) it can cause infection of the fist and possible crippling. Let your attorney do the punching.

IN 1941 REGULAR GASOLINE cost 19.2 cents a gallon. That included the tax.

IF YOU'RE THINKING OF PUTTING ON A HAPPY FACE, remember any licensed doctor can call himself a "plastic surgeon" without having any special training in the field.

PICKPOCKETS JUST LOVE THE PROSPEROUS-LOOKING MAN dressed in conservative loose fitting clothes. Big pockets make the thief's job easier. They do *not* love Levi's.

THE MASSACHUSETTS SUPREME COURT has ruled that employees whose jobs drive them crazy are entitled to collect workmen's compensation. The line forms to the rear.

THE HOTTEST FILM LOCATION IN THE WORLD TODAY isn't Hollywood or the Riviera or the Middle East. It's Illinois. Film directors say they love the state's honest, Midwest flavor, which is something you just can't get in Brazil.

THE SUCCESSFUL SALESMAN has three characteristics that mark him as a winner. He married young, he handles his own money well, and he tends to be even tempered.

EXCESS WEIGHT is the most common nutritional disorder in the United States.

REPUBLICAN AND FORMER DEMO-CRAT JOHN CONALLY grew up in a Texas town called Floresville. It's a small place on the map, but you can find it halfway between Kennedy and Nixon.

WHEN YOU GO TO THE MOVIES IN RUSSIA they won't sell you popcorn, but you can get beer and sandwiches and there's necking in the back row.

COLUMBUS brought pickles to the new world in 1494.

THE AVERAGE EXECUTIVE spends about fifty percent of his time doing his regular work, twenty-five percent doing future-oriented work, fifteen percent doing organization work and one percent doing non-productive work. That means goofing off. "Sorry Jones, I can't talk to you now . . . I'm way behind in my non-productive work and I'll be in the field all day today!"

WHAT TO DO WITH NUCLEAR WASTE? California State Assemblyman Richard Mountjoy has what he considers the perfect plan . . . give it to the Postal Service. Mountjoy says, "The half they don't lose they'll destroy!"

THERE ARE NO QUALIFICATIONS FOR THE JOB of Speaker of the House of Representatives. The speaker, according to law, doesn't even have to be a member of the house to hold the job.

THE WORST SPELLERS IN THE WORLD TODAY are teachers, editors, and journalists. *Journalists?* Well, that's assinein!

Chapter Six

The author's most intimate feelings about his work and his very life are contained in this chapter. Knowing that the unthinking world calls it "trivia," he cannot bring himself to accept it as that. "Trivia is not trivial!" he whines in exasperation, frustration, humiliation, and desperation. "How can I devote my life, my every hour to something that is trivial? This work I do is important. It's needed. It's necessary. The world wants to know how much a pickpocket can earn in Miami, why we call secretaries secretaries, how many men snore at night and what their wives wear to bed." Accepting the truth that somebody has to do this job, somebody has to ferret out the facts and file them for the future in the face of futility, the author struggles to explain his deepest, most secret thoughts on his work. He says, his voice grim with gravity, and just a little gravel. "I give myself willingly to this endeavor because I realize its importance in the history of mankind even if mankind is unkind to the kind of endeavor I willingly give myself!" (*No, I have never run for public office.*)

CHASTITY BELTS ARE STILL BEING MADE in Britain today and worn the world over. David Renwick in London says his chastity belts weigh five pounds each, come equipped with a padlock, two keys, a price tag of about eighty dollars and instructions warning that if the keys are lost the wearer should "use a hacksaw ... *carefully.*"

YOU CAN SPEND two and a half years of your life waiting for your meals to be served.

IN 1885 THE WORLD'S TALLEST BUILDING was the Home Insurance Company of Chicago. All nine stories of it.

HALF THE ESKIMOS IN THE WORLD have never seen an igloo in all their lives.

IN WASHINGTON the Department of Health, Education and Welfare is going along with President Carter's suggestion to streamline government. The HEW rulebook has been cut by more than three hundred pages. There are still 5,696 left, however.

THE WORD "BANJO" comes from the name of the inventor, Joe Sweeney, an Irishman who was so versatile he was called a whole band in himself . . . band Joe.

CONTRARY TO POPULAR BELIEF men are not turned off by women who appear to be easy to get. A man is most attracted to a woman easy for *him* to get but difficult for anybody else.

IF SOMEONE TELLS YOU YOU'RE CRAZY TO LIVE IN THE SUBURBS they may be right. Twice as many tranquilizers are prescribed in the country as in the big cities today.

LONDON'S OFFICE OF POPULATION says men are more likely to suffer heart attacks on a Monday. It's the result of the stress of going back to the grind again. Or overeating over the weekend.

THE EARTH IS FARTHER FROM THE SUN in the summer than in the winter.

EIGHTY-FIVE BILLION IN COIN AND CURRENCY is now in circulation in the USA and nobody knows exactly where it is. Much of it is being held by individuals in private hoards of one hundred dollar bills.

FOR EVERY TEN WOMEN WHO GET A FACE LIFT two or three men get the works as well. Approximately $2,500 will cover a complete job. Around $500 will get you a mini. Your doctor can do it for you now over the weekend.

IT WAS THE DUTCH, NOT THE ENGLISH who first sipped tea. In those days it was used only as a laxative.

CALVIN COOLIDGE WAS KNOWN AS A MAN OF FEW WORDS. He really was. He disposed of his estate in a will which was just one sentence long.

YOU CAN CUT DOWN ON YOUR SMOKING before a stressful situation if you take an Alka Seltzer. Columbia University studies show that smokers who took bicarb before the important meeting or speech or cocktail party, actually smoked 22.7 percent fewer cigarettes.

MEN TAKE MORE TIME investigating a stock before they purchase it than women do.

JAPAN IS THE SAFEST INDUSTRIALIZED NATION in the world. Compared to the United States, Japan has one fifth the murder rate, less than one percent of the robbery rate and about twenty-eight percent of the rate for theft.

IF YOU'RE ON A DIET AND YOU FEEL HUNGER PANGS it may help to know they usually last only ten minutes.

ADOLPH HITLER'S FAVORITE FILM was "King Kong."

MOSCOW'S SUBWAY SYSTEM with its marble columned stations and gilt chandeliers is less than half the size of New York's but it carries more passengers. About five million a day.

LONDON'S CLINK STREET was once the site of a well-known jail. That's why we still call those places "clinks."

IN DUBLIN, IRELAND St. Patrick's Cathedral is a Protestant church.

CLUB SODA IS A FINE STANDBY CLEANER for getting grease spots and wine stains off your clothes. It works even when the soda is flat.

ONLY EIGHTEEN AND A HALF PERCENT of the American drivers today ever use their seat belts.

THOSE LINES THAT RUN FROM YOUR NOSE TO YOUR UPPER LIP are called "philtra." You've had your fill of philtra?

THERE'S ALMOST SEVENTEEN SQUARE FEET OF SKIN on the average female body. Ah, research!

IN DENVER, COLORADO IT'S AGAINST THE LAW to step out of any airplane into the air unless there's an emergency.

ACCORDING TO THE RULES OF THE BRITISH PARLIAMENT, members are expressly forbidden to call each other a jackass. It has been ruled, however, that they may refer to each other as a goose. You silly goose, you!

IF YOU HAVE A WELL GROOMED MOUSTACHE you can figure it costs you $27 a year to keep it that way.

POUND FOR POUND wood is stronger than steel.

NEARLY HALF THE PEOPLE IN THE UPPER STORIES of any skyscraper will get sick on windy days. That's because the buildings tend to sway back and forth as much as three feet.

EIGHTY-FIVE PERCENT OF CHINA'S nine hundred million people are under the age of 25.

SCIENTISTS ARE NOW WORKING on turning newsprint into food. Supposedly the newspaper is an excellent source of carbohydrates. Have a newsburger, but hold the front page.

TESTS CONDUCTED IN DELFT, HOLLAND show that a coconut shell absorbs shock better than your average crash helmet. When you motorcycle around town this weekend, put some coconut in your hat.

PEOPLE HIRED TO FIND RUNAWAY WIVES say the husband is hardly ever able to give such vital statistics as height, weight, or eye and hair color. However, if she drove away in the family car, the husband can always remember the make, year, and model.

YOU ALWAYS THINK AT TOP EFFICIENCY WHEN YOU'RE HORIZONTAL. If you have a difficult problem to solve today you can do it seven-and-a-half times faster lying down on the job. Take your pillow to work.

YOUR DESK, if you have one, reflects your personality. Psychologist Andre J. Brumley says people with neat desks usually have organized minds and mental habits. Messy desks usually reflect a very creative "star quality" type. I'm a star.

JUST BEFORE HE BECAME A FAMOUS NEWS COMMENTATOR, the late Edward R. Murrow changed his first name from Egbert. That's the way it was.

Chapter Seven

This chapter tells the author's entire life story, from his days as a wondrous child who said brilliant things, many of them in those times unprintable, to his first radio shows where he said brilliant things carefully edited, to his current role as chronicler of his times, writer of brilliant things, printable all. (*It isn't that I have cleaned up my act, but rather that the world over the years has systematically lowered its standards.*)

THE AVERAGE PAYCHECK 150 years ago was $5.30.

IF YOU HAVE FOUR-AND-A-HALF MILLION IN TWENTY DOLLAR BILLS now, you have enough there to fill fourteen average suitcases. Check it out. Then get out of town.

ARABIAN MEN GO A LITTLE CRAZY when they find a woman with a double chin.

IT USED TO BE THAT TRAIN NUMBER 147 FROM MOSCOW to the Black Sea made the trip in 21 hours, 39 minutes. The Russians put on a new train number 97 and called it Express Service. The new express train takes 64 minutes longer.

IN VILCABAMBA, EQUADOR everybody lives to be over one hundred. The average age there seems to be one hundred and thirty-eight and some even live to be one hundred and sixty-eight. One man in Vilcabamba is one hundred and thirty-seven now and he says he doesn't feel a day over 95.

THE FOUR SEASONS RESTAURANT in New York City serves forty-seven glasses of wine for every executive martini at lunch.

THEY STILL SHOW SILENT MOVIES IN THAILAND, but live actors stand behind the screen and do the lines.

THE AVERAGE AMERICAN HOUSE-HOLD spends twenty-three percent more on soft drinks than on milk.

KIM DARBY'S REAL NAME is Derby Zerby.

EVERY UNITED STATES PRESIDENT WITH A BEARD was a Republican.

SCIENTISTS GEORG SIMON OHM, ANDRE MARIE AMPERE, AND JAMES WATT introduced "ohms," "amperes," and "watts" to our language.

HAMBURGER will account for half of America's beef supply within the next ten years. America's favorite . . . chocolate, vanilla, and hamburger.

RIO DE JANIERO HAS 512 PLASTIC SURGEONS. No waiting.

ONE PERSON OUT OF EVERY FOUR IN AMERICA today worries about money. The other three *say* they don't.

DESPITE ALL THE REPORTS OF PEOPLE GOING GRAY OVERNIGHT, it never happens that way. It takes months or years to get completely gray. Unless you use a bottle. Then it takes about forty-five minutes.

CROCODILES CANNOT CHEW. Lucky for you. Crocodiles simply break, crunch, and gulp. Occasionally a croc will eat a person but usually they try to avoid them. Gives them gas.

SHARKS HAVE UP TO 36,000 POUNDS OF CRUSHING PRESSURE with their teeth. That's enough power to rip the door off my '67 Cougar.

COMFORT, TEXAS is half way between two little towns named Alice and Louise. A sign outside a motel there invites weary travelers to "Sleep in Comfort between Alice and Louise!"

ABBOTT LABORATORIES HAS DEVELOPED A SNEAKY ASPIRIN. It sneaks past the stomach and is liberated only after reaching the blood, thus avoiding stomach trouble. Testing is going on now at their Montreal labs.

IN THE NICOLAI VAVILOV PLANT BREEDING INSTITUTE in Russia, scientists are playing songs for wheat seeds. The wheat is growing three times as fast with the music. One of the songs they play is "Wheat Georgia Brown."

THE U.S. CIVIL DEFENSE OFFICE says in case of an atomic bomb attack you should shut all doors and windows and never start rumors. Never start a rumor in a bomb blast.

WHEN IT GETS REALLY COLD IN PARIS the Eiffel Tower shrinks by six inches.

THE AVERAGE WORKING WOMAN gets dressed each morning in just sixteen minutes and then spends the rest of the day adjusting it all.

IF YOU NEED A SILENT PARTNER NOW YOU CAN BUY ONE. Silent Partner is an inflatable male dummy that looks just like a real executive dummy. Give him his own office. Discuss secrets with him. Agreeable, quiet and thoroughly dull, Silent Partner is available from 4706 Camp Bowie, Fort Worth, Texas 76107.

IN A YWCA SURVEY OF WOMEN ACHIEVERS, seventy-five percent said they had children and that marriage helped their career advancement.

SATELLITE PICTURES show that India is pushing China around. India is slowly nudging China into the Pacific at the rate of one inch per year.

THE PRE-SALTED TOMATO IS ON THE WAY. An American tomato has been cross-bred now with a Galápagos Islands tomato that grows wild near salt water. The result is a new commercial tomato with a ready-salted taste.

THE CAUSE OF MOST OFFICE MISTAKES is bad penmanship . . . people who write notes other people can't read.

IN THAILAND CLASSICAL MUSIC IS QUIETLY PLAYED as a background to any boxing match.

ACCORDING TO AN OLD VIRGINIA LAW nobody but a political candidate is allowed to practice corruption and bribery.

PEOPLE WILL REMEMBER THE NUMBER OF TIMES YOU SUCCEED. They don't always remember the times you tried and failed. People still remember Ty Cobb who stole ninety-six bases out of 134 tries. That's seventy percent. But almost no one remembers Max Corey who stole fifty-one out of fifty-three bases for ninety-six percent.

WHEN SIR HENRY ROYCE DIED IN 1933 the Rolls Royce monogram RR was changed from red to black.

THERE'S A NEW WRIST WATCH that doesn't merely measure time. It counts your heartbeats as well. Time Computer Inc. says their new watch flashes the time and the pulse rate at the touch of your finger. Now you can tell what time it is and if you're alive.

IT'S EASIER TO LEARN CHINESE THAN SPANISH OR FRENCH. Allan B. Goldenthal, author of the book *Think Chinese, Speak Chinese* says, "Chinese is utterly simplistic when compared to English, German, Russian or Japanese."

WHEN PRESENTED WITH IDENTICAL CASE HISTORIES psychiatrists rarely agree on the nature of the illness.

DR. GAETAN ZAPPALO INSISTS MUSIC CAN BE USED TO CURE AILMENTS. The Italian surgeon says Bach fugues sooth indigestion. Mozart works well on rheumatism. Beethoven treats hernias. Schubert helps you go to sleep when you can't and Handel heals a broken heart.

IF YOU TELEPHONE THE WEATHER CENTER IN MOSCOW you're instructed to write a letter explaining why you want to know what kind of day it will be.

IF YOU MAKE IT TO PARADISE YOU WON'T FIND IT CROWDED. Exactly ten people live in Paradise, North Dakota. It's no Paradise.

IF YOU SEEM TO BE ONLY HALF ALIVE ON THE JOB most of the time there could be good reason for that. Scientists at Dalhousie University in Halifax, Nova Scotia says the human brain may work in 90-minute cycles. Your peak performance comes for just a minute or so every cycle. That means during an average eight-hour day you may be at your mental best for only fifteen or twenty minutes ... and *this* is not one of them.

Chapter Eight

The chapter that finds the author alone at his typewriter, his mind as blank as the paper in the machine is Chapter Eight. Half the book to go and not a thought in his handsome head! Running his strong, heavily veined fingers through his strong, heavily curled hair, he looks at his world through green-hazed eyes, vacant, lost, and alternately dumb. As the twilight darkens the lonely room, his heavily massive chest heaves in a wretched sigh and his thin, but heavily sensuous lips form the inaudible words "H-E-L-P M-E!" (*There's one part in the middle of everything I write when I don't think I can ever finish it. That's when I stop and have a beer. Or two. After that I feel better and then I don't care if I never finish it.*)

CHRISTOPHER COLUMBUS had snow white hair at the age of thirty.

BRITISH SEX EXPERT DR. PIERRE MARSHALL has applied to the government for funds to open a school for love. He says at his institute students will lie around on cushions all day while absorbing the curriculum. But nobody will want to matriculate.

IF YOU'RE A PASSENGER IN A CAR, some insurance company figures say you're safest when you ride with a farmer, a finance company executive, or the manager of a wholesale business. The worst driver to be with is a radio personality (that figures!), a liquor dealer, a professional athlete, or the owner of a Rolls Royce.

IT TAKES EIGHT YARDS OF WOOL to make one Scottish kilt.

IN EGYPT TODAY divorce is on the increase. As one Egyptian woman put it. "There's more to life than cooking, working and taking care of children." In other words, today's Egyptian females don't want to become mummies.

THE BOUNDARY LINE BETWEEN CANADA AND THE USA runs right through the middle of the little town of Rock Island, Quebec. As a result an audience sitting in the local Opera House is in the USA while the players perform in Canada.

THE ENGLISH WORD "GAB" comes from the Gaelic word meaning mouth.

IN SAN JOSE, COSTA RICA if you park illegally they unscrew your number plates and take them away. You get the plates back only when you appear in court and pay a fine.

CONSTRUCTION WORKERS IN RUS-SIA are never told what they're building. It might help if they knew, but they don't know until they're through.

AUSTRALIAN family planners have been trying to teach Aborigine women the basics of contraception by teaching them a song on that subject. They've run into some trouble, however. Some of the women thought they could avoid pregnancy by singing the little song.

AS LATE AS THE 1890s doctors cautioned against taking more than one bath a week lest people lose their magnetism.

IN 1921 THE PRINCE OF WALES was one of the first men in the world to wear a zipper in his pants.

IT'S ILLEGAL to drive more than 2000 sheep down Hollywood Boulevard at any one time.

IF SOMEONE ASKS YOU TODAY TO CREATE A JUXTAPOSITION of two obricu-

laris oris muscles in a state of contraction, you'll
know you're being asked to pucker up.

**A NINE COUNTRY STUDY OF HUS-
BANDS** by the European Community Commis-
sion says British, Dutch, and Danish men make
the best hubbies. Italian husbands are the worst.
Italian men won't wash a dish, won't change
the diapers, won't do the ironing. Italian husbands say women's work is never done . . . by
them.

**THE AYATOLLAH MAY NOT BE THE
AYATOLLAH.** International Intelligence Report says photos of the *real* Ayatollah Khomeini,
from his years of exile in Paris, show he was
missing the middle finger on his right hand.
Photos of the present Ayatollah show all ten
digits.

A DUTCH MERCHANT has the solution
for gold investors who want to show off. Ted
Veenendaal is selling solid gold dinnerware.
Each plate costs around $60,000. Hamburger
Helper looks lousy on it. Mr. Veenendaal admits
his wares aren't for everybody but he says leaders, rock stars, and aging actresses like the stuff
for picnics in the park. A setting for thirty-six
people is in the 5.78 million range. I didn't
buy a set because I told myself it was too
showy.

SCIENTISTS IN INDIA are using oil-eating bacteria to clean up their beaches. A small bottle of the hungry bacteria can clean ten miles of beach. Unlike the chemical oil fighters used by Western governments, the bacteria are non-toxic and biodegradable.

IN BRAZIL NOW THEY'RE GETTING GAS FROM TAPIOCA. The Brazilians aren't having problems digesting pudding. They're getting alcohol from the cassava plant, from which tapioca is made. Tapioca gas is a renewable fuel. When they need more they just plant it.

SPECIALISTS DR. MICHAEL J. COOPER of Kaiser-Permanente Medical Center in Oakland, California and Dr. Maurice M. Aygen of the Toor Heart Institute in Israel have found that transcendental meditation can lower your cholesterol level. The doctors tested twelve patients over an eleven month period and discovered that a regular program of relaxation technique, TM, or some other system like it, can really reduce high cholesterol.

THERE IS AN ENERGY CRISIS in the USA, but in Russia the big problem is soap. There isn't any. A shortage of sulfanol to produce detergent has caused homemakers to grate all the available bar soap. Now there's *no* soap. There are also shortages of bathroom tissue, toothpaste, and shampoo. (*The Soviets have no sulfanol, but there's still plenty of vodcanol.*)

JOSHUA FIT THE BATTLE OF JERI-CHO and the walls came tumbling down. But maybe not from the sound of the Israelites' trumpets as the bible says. Geologist Amos Nur believes earthquakes did in those famous walls. His studies show quakes measuring six to seven on the Richter scale must have occurred about every 200 years along the Dead Sea Rift.

BULLS WILL NOT CHARGE AT YOU ferociously if you're wearing your birthday suit. A farmer in Southern France tried bulls to scare away nudists on his property. The bulls refused to attack. Bulls believe naked people to be harmless animals and leave them alone. Next time you're confronted with a lot of bull take off your clothes.

Chapter Nine

In this chapter the author remembers his first love. Tender. Innocent. Sweet. Clara Louise Munko. The eighth grade. Singing "Side By Side" and "Heart of My Heart" at the upright in the Munko's parlor on Sunday nights. Walking to school. Kicking the leaves. Carrying books. Sitting in the last row of the balcony in the Stoneham Theatre watching "Now Voyager." (*How could anybody named Clara Louise have a forty-two inch bust in the eighth grade?*)

THE WORLD'S POPULATION is growing at a slower rate now than ten years ago, but it's still growing. The population is increasing by 74 million each year or 1 million every five days.

LONDON DOCTOR DAVID CARRICK says if you're out of condition he has a wonder cure for you. It's a dog. Dr. Carrick says it's easy to put off jogging, but much harder to ignore that brown-eyed pup begging for a walk. The doctor says dog walking is safer, too, than jogging since it's less rigorous but still constant exercise.

THAT BAKED POTATO YOU HAVE FOR SUPPER originally sold at fantastic prices in Spain as a sovereign remedy for impotence.

THE SWISS ARE THE WORLD'S BIGGEST SAVERS. A twenty-three nation survey by the International Savings Bank Institute shows the Swiss put away an average of more than $15,000 a year.

THERE ARE MORE THAN 400 MILLION TELEPHONES in operation worldwide. That's a lot of wrong numbers.

THE WINGED BEAN OF ASIA has thirty-seven percent protein in the beans and the roots have ten times more protein than your potato.

A LETTER ASKING FOR CONTRIBUTIONS to the U.S. Olympic Committee was addressed to the World Desk of United Press International. It began, "Dear Mr. Desk."

TO BOW IS TO SHOW COURTESY IN JAPAN, but today proper bowing is a lost art among the young. Mr. Takahashi Torimoto of Osaka has corrected this with his bow-training machine. Students of the bow stand upright inside the contraption and press against a breastplate which then bends their bodies to three different required social positions. Fifteen degrees is used when bowing to colleagues. Thirty degrees is used for welcoming a client or VIP. A forty-five degree bow is reserved for a proper *sayonara*. Now if someone would only invent a "Thank you very much!" machine for the USA.

THERE ARE 25 MILLION RATS IN LIMA, PERU and 5 million people.

GETTING MONEY FROM WASHINGTON is easier than you think. Federal auditors tested the security of government computer systems recently. They created a phony company and submitted a bill for $96,000. The General Services Administration paid it, no questions asked. They submitted another bill and it too was paid. In both cases the GSA, ever on the lookout to save money, subtracted two percent for prompt payment.

NOW IF THEY FIND YOU GUILTY of committing adultery in Greece they will allow you time to get dressed before they haul you in. In the past adulterers were taken naked, or as they were found, to the police station so their guilt could be proved. The Greek Parliament finds every year about 300 couples are taken nude to police stations.

THAILAND'S QUEEN SIRIKIT is highly allergic to pollution, especially exhaust fumes and dust. Bangkok, with its heavy traffic and high humidity, is one of the world's most breathless cities. Thailand's Queen is allergic to Thailand.

IN A THREE WEEK PERIOD ON JAPANESE NETWORK TV critics counted nearly 2,000 killings.

IF YOUR FELLOW WORKERS MUMBLE THAT YOU'RE ALWAYS THROWING A FIT, why not give them what they want. Boston ad exec Stavros Cosmopulos has produced a nine-to-five sponge. Neatly emblazoned on your sponge is the word "FIT." When the boss mumbles and grumbles you pick up your sponge and throw it.

NINETY-SIX PERCENT OF EGYPTS 40 MILLION PEOPLE live squeezed onto only four percent of the land, the long, green strands that flank the Nile.

LONDON is now the world's most expensive city for international travelers. Just four years ago it was 39th on the list. After London comes Vienna, Paris, Frankfurt and Brussels.

THE VICTORIA, CANADA MUNICIPAL COUNCIL has asked its local citizens to approve a law banning chicken chasing before seven AM and after eleven PM.

IN ONE HOUR THE AVERAGE OFFICE WORKER gives off about the same amount of heat as a burning 100 watt light bulb. I've been meaning to speak to you about that.

TWENTY YEARS AGO the man was the bread winner in fifty-six percent of all families. Today men bring home the money in only thirty-four percent of families.

THE HAPPIEST PERSON IN THE USA TODAY is supposed to live in the far West, is twenty-five to thirty-four years old and makes $25,000 a year. I can't give you the complete names and addresses because that wouldn't be right.

YOUR HORSE will never get a cavity. I was worried about that.

THE DOUBLE DOORS on the front of the Manufacturers Hanover International Bank in Miami are made of bronze and cost $13,000.

THERE ARE MORE PSYCHIATRISTS PER PERSON IN WASHINGTON, D.C. than in any other spot in the country. It figures.

IT TAKES THE AVERAGE CHICKEN PLUCKING MACHINE fourteen seconds to de-feather your bird.

IN IDAHO FALLS, IDAHO it's still against the law for anyone over the age of eighty to ride a motorcycle.

THE WALDORF ASTORIA spends $35,000 a year just to keep the chandeliers clean. There are seventy of them.

THE MAN WHO SET THE HIGHEST GROSS INCOME ever amassed in a single year by a private citizen in this country was second-hand furniture dealer, Al Capone.

WILLIAM H. BONNEY was in business for himself in the 1870s. No one called him Mr. Bonney. No one called him W.H. In the twenty-one years he lived they called him Billy the Kid.

PUBLIC BATHS IN ENGLAND during the reign of Henry the Second were called "stews."

THE CITY DUMP in West Covina, California is located on Aroma Drive.

THAT SWISS CHARD IN YOUR GARDEN is not really Swiss chard. It's really one of the many varieties of beet.

THE BOBOLINK is an American bird but it loves to eat Chinese. Rice growers at one time hunted bobolinks because the birds like to dine on the white grain. In fact, the bobolink's other name is Rice Eater.

150 YEARS AGO in all the miles of palace that housed Catherine the Great of Russia, there was only one bathroom. But even then there was an old lady in there with hot towels and a saucer full of rubles.

Chapter Ten

Here is where the author, determined, strong, even willful, takes on Hollywood and tells his personal and often disgusting stories of movie stars long since dead and unable to defend themselves. He purposely shocks here with reports of unbridled lust, longing, lingerie and longitude. The works! He exposes Tinsel Town's blatant heterosexuality, homosexuality, and unrelenting cordiality! Fascinating reading! Hot stuff! The Bergen Record calls it "Primitive writing . . . openly weird." The Maui News gives it One Star and says "Unprintable . . . even filthy!" (*Actually, this chapter has nothing to do with Hollywood and is blatantly dull stuff, which is why I thought the least I could do here was make the opening interesting for you. The*

Bergen Record and the Maui News never said any of those things. On the other hand, I know for a fact there's an awful lot of cordiality going around on Sunset!)

IN THE TROPICS the Kissing Bug is the kissin' cousin of the bed bug and when the Kissing Bug kisses, like Dracula, he never misses.

NORTH CAROLINA just loves French fried *sweet* potatoes.

IF YOU SUFFER FROM GENITO-FEMORAL NEUROPATHY your jeans are too tight. Wranglers can be stranglers.

CALIFORNIA LEADS ALL OTHER STATES in the reporting of UFOs.

THAT PERENNIAL PLANT THE RHUBARB has been known to reproduce new stalks every year for up to fifty years from the original planting.

SOVIET AUTHORITIES have started a T-shirt superiority push aimed at taking over the market from America. Approved slogans for the Russian T's include "The Communist Party and the People Are One" and "Glory to Labor."

THE WORLD'S POPULATION is growing at a slower rate now than ten years ago, but it's still growing. The population is increasing by 74 million each year or one million every five days.

THE DOLLAR MAY TAKE A BEATING THESE DAYS, but the Hamburg Institute for Economic Research in West Germany says it's still used in fifty-two percent of all the transactions in the world. The German mark is second at fourteen percent and the French franc and the English pound are tied for third at seven percent.

AMERICAN LEADERS believe now that older workers have better attendance records than younger people and they're much more productive. A survey done for the Corporate Committee for Retirement Plannning says most execs now believe older employees should stay on as long as they're healthy.

A NEW DRUG, PHENOXYBENZAMINE, can help relieve the serious problem of enlarged prostate. Doctors at Hadassah University Hospital in Jerusalem say the medication can be an alternative to surgery.

DISCO MUSIC HAS STARTED RIOTS in the USA, but a South African company intends to use it to stop them. The company says it will market a special anti-riot truck equipped with loudspeakers. Once they turn on those disco hits, the theory goes, the protestors will stop protesting and start to boogie. If that doesn't work the truck is equipped with tear gas.

DR. ANNER ZIV of Tel Aviv University says today's psychologists are so serious they're afraid to laugh or use humor. He thinks a little laughter might get us off the couches faster.

OF THE WORLD'S more than 4 billion people fifty-eight percent are Asians, thirteen percent are African, ten percent Latin Americans, nine percent Europeans, five percent Russians, and five percent North Americans.

AT LAST COUNT there were thirty-seven major and minor wars taking place around the world.

TYCOONS, BUSINESSMEN, AND BAKERS are all good lovers. At least they are in Italy—professors at Rome University say so.

BRAZIL'S FAMOUS KILLER BEES aren't killers anymore. The killers have been mating with kinder, nicer, home-loving bees and the result is a reformed "born again" bee.

THE COLDEST TOWNS IN THE WORLD are Verkyoyanks and Oymyakon in Soviet Siberia. Temperatures there drop to minus ninety-six degrees Farenheit. I wonder what the wind-chill factor is?

A COMPANY IN LONDON that orders items from Taiwan has had a slight problem with 50,000 tea towels. The towels were to commemorate William the Conqueror. But instead of reading "William the First, Duke of Normandy," each tea towel was carefully inscribed "William the First, DUCK of Normandy." The British company is now explaining to the Taiwanese the difference between a duck and a duke.

MORE THAN A MILLION MOVIES have been made everywhere in the world since Thomas Edison first filmed a sneeze back in 1893.

THE LETTERS IN BVD stand for Bradley, Voorhees, and Day, the founders of the company.

THE SOUTH KOREANS work harder than anybody else in the world. They put in a fifty-hour work week. They're followed by the Swiss and Czechs who log more than forty-three hours a week. A study by the International Labor Organization shows Americans and Britons work harder than Japanese, the French toil more than the Germans and the Danes take life easy.

A SURVEY OF 150 SECRETARIES shows praise and recognition from the boss are more important than a raise. West German psychologist Jean Werner Sommer says so and she says many bosses fail to realize they can encourage their secretaries to be more productive by noticing their work. *"Gee, Priscilla, you use Liquid Paper better than anybody I've ever seen!"*

THE TIMES THEY ARE A-CHANGING. This year's college freshman class is more materialistic. Today's student is interested in power and status. Sixty-three percent of students say "being very well off financially" is their top goal now.

CANADIAN RESEARCHERS say they've developed a drug that may reverse the effects of cancer. NED-137 they say stimulates the body's natural defense to reject cancerous tissue.

WHEN AN AMERICAN EXECUTIVE was interviewing people for his new London office recently, he had job applications with all the usual information. One middle-aged British woman won a job when she honestly answered a question regarding marital status. She wrote "So so!"

IN TORONTO, CANADA city official June Rowlands has introduced an ordinance that would prevent people earning above a certain amount each year from living in city-run low cost housing. The amount you can still make and live in low cost Toronto apartments is ... $24,000. That's low income!

IF YOU INTEND TO SAVE MONEY and energy today by bringing back the horse and buggy, you should know your sixteen passenger carriage costs $10,000. Your coachman will cost eight to ten thou a year ... (those black top hats are expensive). Also your current model horse, broken and ready to hitch, will set you back about $1,500.

PROFESSOR HANS REUTER of Cologne, Germany says one clove of garlic a day keeps cholesterol away. And everybody else. Reuter says there are fewer cases of hardening of the arteries in China, Greece, Russia, and India because they eat garlic.

IF YOUR DOOR CHIME ONLY CHIMES "DING DONG" you're out of tune with the chimes. Melody Time from Scovill's Nutone Division has a new chime that plays "Auld Lang Syne," "Joy to The World," "Battle Hymn of the Republic," and twenty others. I wonder if I could get something simple for the back door like "Hail to The Chief?"

A TEN YEAR STUDY OF 122,000 JAPA-NESE MEN, aged forty and over, shows a lower death rate from prostrate cancer among those who eat green and yellow vegetables daily. The vitamin A content may be the reason.

BRIGHAM YOUNG UNIVERSITY sociologist Dr. David Cherrington says his studies show the younger the worker is today the less he or she thinks that pride in workmanship is important.

THE AVERAGE CIGARETTE SMOKER costs employers an extra $500 a year. A pipe smoker costs an additional $900 a year. The cigarette smoker wastes thirty minutes a day lighting up and the pipe fanatic can spend even more time cleaning, lighting, and re-lighting.

IF YOU GET A TOOTHACHE while you're touring through China you'll find an eager dentist who will pull out your ailing tooth, drill it, and fill it outside your mouth and then pop it back into your surprised jaw.

WHEN YOUR JAPANESE STEER REACHES THE AGE OF THREE it's of legal drinking age. From that time on the animal gets two quarts of beer a day. That's so Japanese steaks will be properly marbled. *"I'll have the shrimp cocktail, the baked potato, and the Japanese steak. No, I don't want it on a platter . . . just put it in a mug!"*

Chapter Eleven

This is the department in the book filled with photographs depicting various, thrilling, happy, loving, or embarrasing moments in the author's life. First, naturally, a shot of the author naked as the day he was born, taken naked on the day he was born. Adorable! Also here you'll see snaps of the author age five with his grandmother stealing small toys from the F.W. Woolworth store in downtown Woburn, Massachusetts. The little tyke! And of course, Granny could never say no to him! Next, a fine row of out-of-focus photos taken during the author's school days, showing him on the baseball field, winning letters for sport after sport at Stoneham High, and finally a rather sharp shot of him being arrested for stealing small toys. Also included are pictures of the author in therapy sessions in a Morris chair, long before the advent of couches, and stretched out on the living room floor at 7 Ledge Street listening to the wireless, long before the advent of television or the Bendix washing machine which looked like a television. And then, of course, there are included photos of this young, sensitive, dynamic child at the age of eleven seated at his maple desk in his maple chair eating maple sugar and writing in long hand his first book, the story of a young, sensitive, dynamic tyke arrested for stealing small toys. (*Even then he wrote the truth!*)

POLICE IN THE UNITED STATES issue about 82,000 citations every day. Quietly paying the fine may be your best bet. When traffic tickets are challenged in court, two-thirds of the cases are decided in favor of the gendarmes.

A SURVEY OF SOME 2,800 EXECUTIVES by the American Management Association shows fifty-four percent less than minimal satisfaction with their positions.

IF YOU'RE ACTIVE OFF THE JOB you'll live longer than the person who just loafs around. People who are physically active on their own time live 3.8 years longer than those who just put their feet up and read annual reports.

IN THE AMAZON REGION some tarantulas grow so large they catch birds.

IF YOU WANT TO STOP SMOKING GET MARRIED. If you want to start, get a divorce. Studies show that divorced or separated people are more likely to smoke than those who are married and living with their spouses.

JULY AND DECEMBER are the two peak months for murder. During summer vacation and Christmas people are with those most likely to kill them; relatives, friends, and drinking companions.

IF YOU'VE EVER BEEN JABBED WITH A HYPODERMIC NEEDLE you've had a silicone implant. Silicone is used to coat the needles and cut down on the pain. With each shot a little bit of the stuff is left inside you.

ABOUT EIGHT MILLION JUNK CARS are recycled for their steel in the USA each year. That's a lot of '67 Cougars.

NEXT TIME THE BOARD OF DIREC-TORS MEETING gives you the twitches, take a walk. Chicago physician Dr. Herbert De Vries says a fifteen minute walk can alleviate tension better than a tranquilizer. He says, "Modest exercise calms nervous tension and improves body tone."

THE REASON AMERICANS DON'T LIVE AS LONG AS OTHER PEOPLE around the world is retirement. Nutritionist Dr. Jean Mayer says in other countries there is no forced retirement. An older person's work is necessary, their advice is solicited, their wisdom respected.

YOU CAN DRINK MORE BOOZE on the supersonic Concorde and not get as drunk as you could on other planes. Cabin pressure is lower.

THE PEOPLE'S REPUBLIC OF CHINA has a birth control pill for men. They say it's 99.8 percent effective. In fact, during the tests of ten thousand men over a period of four years, not one of them became pregnant.

TIMEX has introduced a camera that produces 3-D photographs. With four lenses it combines images to create the illusion of depth in a print or slide. Like their famous watches, it takes a licking and keeps on clicking.

GRINGLISH IS NOW "SPOKE" IN MANY PLACES around the world. Travelers find signs in East Berlin hotel cloakrooms reading "Please hang yourself here!" A Dutch bulb catalogue offers mail order buyers "a speedy execution." A bread bakery in Bombay says "We are number one loafers...best in whole town." An Istanbul hotel room sign reads "To call room service, please to open door and call room service." And a Mexican hotel requests "Please hang your order before retiring on your doorknob."

SCOTCH, GIN, AND VODKA were discovered accidentally by ancient researchers trying to come up with some new perfumes.

IN INDIA YOUR HAMBURGER STAND sells lamb-burger instead.

A CANADIAN PENNY costs two pennies to make.

IF YOU'RE PART OF A HIJACKING be inconspicuous if you can. Experts insist it's the conspicuous travelers who are likely to be dealt with first if things get rough.

EIGHT YEARS AGO MOST PEOPLE BE-LIEVED that hard work would lead to success. Today the majority believe you have to know somebody or be very lucky. (*If you're lucky enough to know somebody and they help you to be successful you still have to work hard!*)

NICE GUYS NOT ONLY FINISH LAST, THEY DIE FIRST. So says Professor John Brantner of the University of Minnesota. He says those who survive longest in this old world are the fault finders.

VASOPRESSIN RESTORES YOUR MEM-ORY if you forget things a lot. Amnesiacs and normal patients who use it as a nasal spray (three puffs a day) remember everything. In Spain, four amnesia patients reported memory recovery within five to nine days. Just remember where you put the stuff.

A MAN-MADE COMPUTER with a memory as good as a human brain, able to store up to one hundred billion items of information, would occupy most of a building the size of the Empire State Building and would use electrical energy at the rate of one billion watts.

SOME SNORING HAS BEEN MEA-SURED AT SIXTY-NINE DECIBLES. That's the same level for the noises of a jack hammer on a construction job. Or an angry lion with a thorn in his paw. By the way, there is one sure-fire method of overcoming snoring problems. Sleep all by yourself. Just your blue blanket and your matching jammies with the little red hearts. And close your door.

IF YOU HAVE RUBBER BANDS AND YOU WANT THEM TO LAST forever store them in your office refrigerator. They like to be cool.

MAINE HAS MORE FOREST LAND than any other state. Ay-yup!

GASAHOL was used as a fuel over one hundred years ago. The original Model T Ford was designed to run on gas or alcohol or a combination of both.

ON MARCH 16, 1876 Nell Saunders defeated Rose Harland in America's first female boxing match. The winner's prize was a silver butter dish.

WHEN THE MAN IN THE WHITE HOUSE TAKES A SHOWER after a jog through the Rose Garden he can thank Andrew Jackson. Jackson had the first warm and cold shower bath installed at the First Family's home.

FORTY TONS OF FERTILIZER ARE SPREAD EACH YEAR ON CAPITOL HILL. By groundskeepers, not by Congressmen.

Chapter Twelve

Now we encounter the brief but all too fleeting time in this book when the author remembers dancing on the lawn in a chicken suit with the obscenely rich Long Island duckling, Lorna. Finger bowls filled with Dubonnet, they munched on strawberry mousse and worshiped the moonlight in the back seat of his Studebaker President, which Lorna noted looked exactly like the front seat of his Studebaker President. No one could ever tell which way that car was going. And no one could tell where the author was going. He had assumed it would be fame, fortune, and fooling around. The three F's. Fool! Little did he know Chapter Thirteen would follow Chapter Twelve and night would follow day and he would follow Lorna. Fallow

fellow! (*It was then that I untangled Loina . . .
I had already moved to Brooklyn and could not
speak correctly . . . anyhow, I untangled her
from my lorns and backed up the Studebaker
and then drove it forward and sadly, no one
knew the difference.*)

BANANAS CAN CAUSE MORE TOOTH DECAY than sweets. Bananas drive cavities bananas.

HARES HAVE FUR AND CAN SEE AT BIRTH. Rabbits are born blind and hairless. Not hareless, hairless!

BOWLERS WITH SORE THUMBS LOVE POTATOES. Well-known pro-bowlers are sticking sore thumbs into potatoes to get them well again. Mark Roth says it works but he's embarrassed to ask the Holiday Inn for an uncooked potato.

THE DUCHESS OF BEDFORD HAS HAD A FACELIFT. When asked why, she told reporters, "I just love restoring old things!"

DOCTORS SAY, if you go to bed hungry, you'll live seven years longer. Seven long, hungry years.

PLAYING THE PIANO can use more calories than gymnastic exercises. If you want to lose weight play some Ethelbert Nevins.

TAKE YOUR PAIN TO SPAIN. Researchers at Sweden's University of Gotenburg have found that arthritis patients suffer less and improve more rapidly in a warm, dry climate such as Spain's. Cold, icy weather slows down any improvement.

RESEARCHERS AT MEXICO'S UNIVERSITY OF AMERICAS have developed soy milk at about fifteen cents a quart. It can be stored without refrigeration for up to two months. Two months old soy? Oiy!

DUBUQUE, IOWA has more millionaires per capita than in any other place in the USA. They really bring home the bacon in Dubuque.

A PICKPOCKET IN MIAMI can earn $20,000 a year.

DR. SANFORD WRIGHT of Washington has obtained a patent for an invention that allows you to write something with one hand and then see what you've written on a miniature computer attached to your opposite wrist. From now on your right hand *will* know what your left is doing.

THE EYES OF DISHONEST AND DECEITFUL PEOPLE aren't nearly as shifty as those of the thoroughly honest, dedicated person. Look into it.

EXECUTIVES WHO HAVE HEART ATTACKS get back to work sooner and generally fare much better than people in their employ.

WITH THE ACCENT ON DIET TODAY, brewers are turning out lighter beers. The light brews have taken over one third of the market. Schlitz is working up fruit-flavored beer. Cherry, orange, lemon, and gusto.

THE AVERAGE HOUSEWIFE IN THIS COUNTRY cooks 57,000 meals during her life

time. That's an awul lot of burgers and maca-
roni.

INSTANT COFFEE dates back some sixty-
eight years. Blanke's soluble coffee was adver-
tised in April, 1912.

SHAKESPEARE may have written the
King James edition of the bible. If you check
the forty-sixth word from the beginning of
Psalm Forty-six you'll find it's *shake*. Check the
forty-sixth word from the end of the psalm and
you'll find it's *spear*. The translation of the King
James version was completed on Willaim Shakespeare's forty-sixth birthday.

YELLOWSTONE was the first national
park in the world.

RHODE ISLAND calls itself America's
first vacationland. The claim goes back to 1524
when the Italian explorer Giovanni da Ver-
razano sailed the coast. He found Narragansett
Bay so pleasant he stayed a fortnight. That's
the first two-week vacation on record.

DOCTORS IN SWEDEN say they've invented a nasal birth control spray for women.
It's taken once a day and they say it's 100% effective. I say please don't sneeze.

IF YOU HEAD FOR THE HILLS, the highest levels, the chances are good you may avoid a heart attack. Men have better chances of avoiding heart disease today by living in high altitudes above sea level. It seems the reduced oxygen tension of life on the hills has the same effect as increased exercise. If you live in a valley you'd better jog a lot.

ENGLISH MUFFINS are an American invention. Danish pastry is called Vienna Bread in Denmark.

PROFESSOR PHIL KLASS of Pennsylvania State University predicts that in the next century there will be not two, but six or seven sexes.

ONE OUT OF EVERY EIGHT MEN SNORES. Snoring men outnumber snoring women twelve to one.

THE BIGGEST SELLING CANDIES OF ALL TIME happen to be Lifesavers. If all the Lifesavers sold from 1923 to the present were stacked on top of each other, the hole in the middle would be more than a million miles deep.

A BAT can eat 1,000 insects in just one hour. If it wants to.

THE AVERAGE CHILD now costs parents $55,784 by the time he or she is eighteen. That doesn't include maternity ward charges or the cost of a college education.

A CHINESE DENTIST has extracted more than 30,000 teeth by finger pressing at acupuncture points. Dr. King Hsueh-pin uses no anesthesia. He says his patients feel only slight pain, lose less blood and ninety-seven percent of the extractions cause no damage to the surrounding tissue. All this from laying a finger aside of your tooth.

IF YOU HAVE ROSE FEVER, you're not allergic to roses. Or even people named Rose. You're allergic to grass and tree pollens. Roses, either kind, won't bother you.

BOOK SALES in 1979 totalled more than five and three-quarter billion dollars. Reading is *not* a lost art and Irving Wallace and his entire family thank you.

PEOPLE IN ALL WALKS OF LIFE THINK SEX IS HARMFUL to health. Twenty percent of all American farmers think so and so do ten percent of all American secretaries.

ALL NIGHT TELEVISION VIEWING is up by six percent. The 7-11 stores say a full twenty-five percent of their business is done overnight now. The Bell System claims telephone business calls between 11 PM and 8 AM have gone up fifty percent. I'm not about to tell you what other business is carried on after 11 PM in the still of the night, but *it's* up fifty percent too.

Chapter Thirteen

In this chapter the author recalls his days of song writing, fitting words to music, making America sing with his ditties. He always wrote ditties. Delightful ditties. Sometimes depressing ditties, which are very difficult, but always ditties. About love. And life. And love life. And life without love. And windmills in your mind. Or anything to make a buck. (*This, of course, was the famous time in my life when I wrote "I Want To Touch Your Nose!" . . . thank you very much! . . . a song you just may remember goes something like this . . .*

I need to touch your nose
In the morning, behind your door

I need to touch your knees
In the evening, even more

I need to touch the floor
I need to press my shoulder to your thigh

Oh me, oh my ... oh me, oh my
Why must it be? You next to me
Me by your side, your side by me

I need to touch your foot
your toe, you know ... don't you know?

If you help me, hold me, touch me, love me
If the door is closed in the shadow of my
      mind

If I'm with you, beside you, I'll never walk
away and let you go ... I'll watch you
breathe and hold your heel
Kiss your thumb and kneel and say

Stop me from shakin' ... keep me wakin'
and makin' your morning bacon ...
Most of all ... baby ... most of all
This touching world knows ...

I need to touch your nose,
I need to touch your nose,
I never wanted to touch any nose the way
I want to touch your nose

I gotta touch your nose ... even in
repose ... I gotta touch your nose ...
Oh babe!)

VOTERS WHO DESCRIBE THEM-SELVES AS "INDEPENDENT" actually vote for the same party year after year. University of California political scientists say nearly one third of the thirty-five percent of the electorate who describe themselves as Independent vote Democratic most of the time. Another third votes Republican on most occasions.

RODEO RIDERS WEAR PANTY GIR-DLES. They protect against pelvic and leg injuries. Football stars are also into girdles now. The Oklahoma Cowboys use them to prevent hamstring injuries. Saddle up Old Paint, grab the ball, but don't forget your Playtex.

THE FIRST WORDS SPOKEN BY PAUL WILLIAMS when he was introduced to Mickey Rooney . . . "I've always looked up to you!"

THE ANSWER TO STRESS may be as simple as counting your beans. Jerome Techtman of Portland, Oregon says if he gets disturbed he sits right down and opens an eight-ounce can of beans. Then he counts each one. As he counts, his troubles vanish. So, count your blessings if you want to, but when you're disturbed make sure you count your beans.

DOCTORS SAY when the bones in each finger joint are pulled apart, a thin fluid moves into the area. That creates a low pressure zone causing bubbles to form and collapse. That collapse is what makes your knuckles crack.

IF YOU'RE CAUGHT DRINKING A MARTINI IN PAKISTAN, you'll get eighty lashes and six months in jail.

SINGING TO YOUR HOUSE PLANTS may help them grow, but having them blessed can make them fat and sassy. In a recent experiment, two seeds were planted at the same time. One was prayed over daily by a clergyman. The other was left alone. After one month, the blessed plant was three times taller than the unblessed one. So, sing to your plants if you must, but you'd better sing "How Great Thou Art."

YOU CAN GET MARRIED IN PEKING, CHINA if you want to, but you can't go to bed for at least six months. No, it's not some kind of weird regulation. *The People's Daily* says there's a shortage of beds and newlyweds now have to wait half a year. If you're a young couple in China today, you get a "married furniture coupon" when you get hitched. Six months later they give you the bed.

FLIRTING IS GOOD FOR YOUR HEALTH! Cincinnati psychiatrist Dr. E. Richard Dorsey says flirting is good for the psyche, especially good when it pays off. The doctor adds that "the objective of flirting is to attract others, usually of the opposite sex, and often with sex as the goal." Just remember, you read it here first.

THE HEAD OF VENEZUELA'S POSTAL SYSTEM says reforms made under the Social Christian party government have now made it possible for a crosstown letter in Caracas to be delivered in just eight days! That's good. It used to take twenty-one days.

THE WEST GERMAN RESEARCH MINISTRY has warned citizens not to disturb government workers on Mondays. The ministry explains that after a weekend away from the office, civil servants aren't very . . . civil.

A WENDY'S TRIPLE CHEESEBURGER gives you 1,040 calories.

THE AVERAGE AMERICAN eats about seventy pound of tomatoes each year.

WOMEN WITH A LOT OF MONEY to spend are leaner than those with less money around the mansion. For men it's the reverse. As men get up the pay ladder they gain weight. Those two martini lunches do it. However, if a man goes sky high in salary he suddenly becomes a prince again; handsome, trim, and slim.

IF A MAN WANTS TO BE HAPPILY MARRIED he should propose to a plump woman. Anthropologist Anne Scott Beller says fat women are sexier, cuddlier, and more fun to be with.

THE WORD "SECRETARY" comes from the word "secret." It used to be that a secretary wrote down the very personal, private thoughts of the boss.

IF YOU PUT YOUR MONEY IN A SOVI-ET SAVINGS BANK today you'll get two to three percent interest.

CARL SANDBERG went to West Point. But only for a short time. He left after he flunked English.

LONG LUNCH BREAKS ARE GOOD FOR YOU. Dr. Sidney Weissman calls them a "needed break from responsibility." The doctor says the therapeutic value of lunch is as important as the nutritional value.

LEFTIES ARE SUPERIOR TO RIGHT-IES in auditory and music processing ability. Researchers discovered this by testing people, both right- and left-handed, with various musical tones. They kept changing the pitch. The lefties never made a mistake. The righties sometimes couldn't hear the difference. All the tones sounded alike to them. So, if you're left-handed, you may be a musical genius.

A SURVEY OF CURRENT THINKING ON SEXUALITY conducted by the journal, *Medical Aspects of Human Sexuality*, says television is not exactly an aphrodisiac. Over two thirds of the psychiatrists polled agreed that chronic TV watching reduces those romantic interludes. It's all Johnny Carson's fault.

PSYCHOLOGISTS say most people would rather talk to one another at right angles instead of face to face.

IN FINLAND people eat more fat than Americans do, but their incidence of colon cancer is much lower. The Finns have a greater intake of dietary fiber.

A UNIVERSITY OF CALIFORNIA STUDY shows that the person most likely to be working for humanitarian causes and world peace today isn't the young college student. It's your grandmother. The most politically active people in the United States today are grandmothers.

DURING WORLD WAR II the Russians were given some Studebaker trucks. They were so impressed they now call all trucks "Studebakers." When a young Russian wants to say "So long!" he says "Keep on Studebaking!"

IF YOU WANT TO KEEP PAINS FROM YOUR BACK and you're young enough, Dr. Paul Brand says sit cross-legged at least fifteen minutes a day. That position, common in India, causes full rotation of the hips. Dr. Brand says people in India seldom if ever have painful arthritis.

Chapter Fourteen

The ending. The final curtain. The swan song. The wrap. This is the part of every book where the author brings all his characters together, each of them suspicious, of course, and then for the next twenty-seven pages brilliantly, and in insidious detail, tells the reader who done it. Was it Loina? Or Lorna? Was it Clara Louise? Or any of the Munkos? Was it the author's grandmother? And what about F.W. Woolworth? Did the aliens do it? With a BAR? In a Studebaker? Or a Bendix? (*I have such a headache just thinking about it all! You see, as I write this I have no idea what the end is. And I know I have to have an end. I'm sure I have this headache because of my lack of end. Oh well. If I can't think of the ending today I'll try to think about it tomorrow. After all, tomorrow is another day!*)

KISSING IS UNHEALTHY and should be discouraged between consenting adults. Or anybody else. That's what the *Chinese Workers Daily* says. Shaking hands or a smart salute is much preferred.

SOUTH KOREA has about 385,000 cars but last year they had 65,117 accidents.

IF YOU'RE WONDERING HOW MANY YEARS YOU HAVE LEFT you can figure it out the way the life insurance people do. Subtract your current age from 80, multiply the result by 7. Then divide that by 10. However, the experts say if you're more than 70, nobody can make a prediction on the years you have left.

THERE ARE AROUND 200,000 MILLIONAIRES in America today. That's one out of every 1200 people. So, if you aren't one, you probably know one. I know a lot of people who *think* they're millionaires, but they all have car payments.

BLARNEY BELIEVERS ARE BIG SPENDERS. A study conducted in Palo Alto, California found that when people were "sweet talked" with the line "I wish more of the people I met were as interested in their fellowman as you appear to be!" they contributed to the Red Cross much more generously than their non-pitch counterparts.

THE SOCIETY OF JIM SMITHS is an organization with close to 1,000 members worldwide, all named Jim Smith. That includes four women. The founder of the Society of Jim Smiths is Jim Smith.

DON'T LOOK SUSPICIOUS IN LONDON. Police there can arrest you if they feel you are *about to commit* a crime. If you're deemed suspicious . . . into the slammer.

FOR TOOTHACHE RELIEF rub your hand with an ice cube. According to researchers at Montreal's General Hospital and McGill University, ice in the hand will stop pain in the mouth everytime.

A LIFE SENTENCE IN ENGLAND today is running about nine and a half years. The London Times says some lifers get out after as little as two years behind bars. That's a short, sweet life.

SOLAR ONE, THE WORLD'S FIRST SOLAR POWERED AIRCRAFT got off the ground way back in December of 1978. Not *very* far off the ground, but off the ground at least. Two feet.

THE BRITISH NOW PUT THE KETTLE ON and settle back at night to watch X-rated movies in their very own living rooms on TV. Not pay TV, but regular TV. "I say, Pussycat Theatre follows the Muppets tonight at 9!"

NOW WE KNOW WHAT'S WRONG WITH YOUR SEX LIFE. It's your chair. Dr. G. Granjean of the Institute of Industrial Psychology in Zurich says badly adjusted chairs can drain you of thirty to forty percent of your day's energy. The doctor says that can really make it difficult to carry on a normal, or even abnormal, love life in those supposedly romantic evening hours. Put a pillow in your recliner and put some Vitamin E behind each ear.

WHEN YOUR MATE GRINDS HIS OR HER TEETH while sleeping it could be those late nights at the office were really nights on the town. Dr. Ernest Hartman of Tufts University Medical School says nipping before napping can cause bruxism. That's plain, old-fashioned teeth grinding. Just two cocktails are enough to cause that nightly grind. If the problem continues on a regular basis, it can be very damaging to the teeth. However, it takes a lot of Manischewitz to wear your teeth down to the nubs. Sammy Davis told me that.

ONE HEALTHY HANDFUL OF PEA-NUTS contains over 200 calories.

AMERICA NOW HAS EDIBLE GREET-ING CARDS. The cards are actually card-like chocolate bars with messages on them for birthdays or anniversaries. Each chocolate comes with a small tube of gel so you can write your name on top. "F-a-t-t-y."

TODAY THE NUMBER ONE INGREDI-ENT FOR HAPPINESS is an automobile. Just a few short years ago when Americans were asked what the essential ingredient was in a good life, they unanimously said "Children!" *Environmental Action* magazine says that's no longer the case. Kids are okay today, but four-on-the-floor and a tank of gas spells happiness now.

IF SOMEONE SUGGESTS MAGNETS TO RELIEVE YOUR HEADACHE you'd probably be drawn in some other direction. But Dr. Khoe, President of Acupuncture Research Institute says magnets, depending on size and strength, can be used to relieve pain, cure illness, and even break bad habits. Apply two magnets and call me in the morning.

A GROUP OF MUSICIANS in Charlotte, North Carolina today specializes in re-creating the sounds of the Beatles, Rolling Stones, and other rock groups of the 60s. Pat Walters says someone told him his group was sponging off others. Walters agreed and promptly named his outfit The Spongetones.

SOON YOU CAN HAVE A LASAGNA SHAKE OR A STEAK SODA. If you want one. The Army has developed a method for reducing food to tiny particles that can be frozen, thawed, and made into a liquid that retains its flavor. Army researchers created the process for soldiers whose jaws have to be wired during recuperation from accidents or surgery. The

Army is so smart. They'll do anything to find another way to serve SOS.

A BARBERSHOP IN HOUSTON calls itself "The Best Little Hairhouse in Texas!"

About the Author

Jim Aylward's humorous slant on the news is well known from his syndicated newspaper column "Jim Aylward's Journal" and his top rated New York radio programs on WRFM.

He is the author of *You're Dumber in the Summer*, a book of fun facts for young readers.

He has a vivid and sometimes livid imagination, as shown in the chapter openings here, purportedly all based on his real life.

Jim Aylward is six feet, four inches, weighs 180 pounds, and is in need of complete bed rest.

GREAT TRIVIA BOOKS
FROM WARNER BOOKS

THE COMPLETE UNABRIDGED SUPER TRIVIA ENCYCLOPEDIA
by Fred L. Worth (V96-905, $3.50)
Xavier Cugat's theme song? The bestseller of 1929? Miss Hungary of 1936? Here's more than 800 pages of pure entertainment for collectors, gamblers, crossword puzzle addicts and those who want to stroll down memory lane. It asks every question, answers it correctly, solves every argument.

HOLLYWOOD TRIVIA
by David P. Strauss & Fred L. Worth (V95-492, $2.75)
Spotlighting the characters that made Hollywood happen, here are thousands of film facts that will delight and surprise you. Who was buried wearing vampire gear? Who stood on a box to appear taller than his leading lady? Why couldn't Clark Gable secure the leading role in *Little Caesar?* Almost 400 pages of fact and history.

CELEBRITY TRIVIA
by Edward Lucaire (V95-479, $2.75)
Crammed with gossip galore, this book was written with the name-dropper in all of us in mind. It's loaded with public and private memorabilia on actors, writers, rock stars, tyrants—and the scandalous facts they probably wouldn't want you to know. From Napoleon to Alice Cooper, anyone who has caught the public eye is fair game.

THIRTY YEARS OF ROCK 'N' ROLL TRIVIA
by Fred L. Worth (V91-494, $2.50)
Who thought up the name Chubby Checker? Who was paid $10,000 *not* to appear on the Ed Sullivan Show? Who made his television debut with his fly open? A fascinating and colorful compendium of pop memorabilia for both the casual fan and serious afficianado.